Let's Do Math!

Measurements

**Sara Pistoia and
Piper Whelan**

LET'S READ

AV2
BY WEIGL™

ADDED VALUE • AUDIO VISUAL

www.av2books.com

LET'S READ

AV²
BY WEIGL™
ADDED VALUE • AUDIO VISUAL

Go to **www.av2books.com**, and enter this book's unique code.

BOOK CODE
F892698

AV² by Weigl brings you media enhanced books that support active learning.

MAI

3 2401 00910 285 8

AV² provides enriched content that ~~supports~~ ~~complements~~ this book. Weigl's AV² books strive to create inspired learning and engage young minds in a total learning experience.

Your AV² Media Enhanced books come alive with...

 Audio
Listen to sections of the book read aloud.

 Video
Watch informative video clips.

 Embedded Weblinks
Gain additional information for research.

 Try This!
Complete activities and hands-on experiments.

 Key Words
Study vocabulary, and complete a matching word activity.

 Quizzes
Test your knowledge.

 Slide Show
View images and captions, and prepare a presentation.

... and much, much more!

Published by AV² by Weigl
350 5th Avenue, 59th Floor New York, NY 10118
Website: www.av2books.com

Library of Congress Cataloging-in-Publication Data

Names: Pistoia, Sara- author. | Whelan, Piper- author.
Title: Measurement / Sara Pistoia and Piper Whelan.
Description: New York, NY : AV2 by Weigl, [2017] | Series: Let's do math! | Includes index.
Identifiers: LCCN 2016003573 (print) | LCCN 2016008558 (ebook) | ISBN 9781489651105 (hard cover : alk. paper) | ISBN 9781489651112 (soft cover : alk. paper) | ISBN 9781489651129 (Multi-User eBook)
Subjects: LCSH: Measurement--Juvenile literature. | Physical measurements--Juvenile literature. | Mathematics--Juvenile literature.
Classification: LCC QA465 .P5524 2017 (print) | LCC QA465 (ebook) | DDC 530.8--dc23
LC record available at http://lccn.loc.gov/2016003573

Printed in the United States of America in Brainerd, Minnesota
1 2 3 4 5 6 7 8 9 0 20 19 18 17 16

2

072016
210716

Project Coordinator: Piper Whelan
Art Director: Terry Paulhus

The publisher acknowledges iStock and Getty Images as the primary image suppliers for this title.

Let's Do Math!

Measurements

In this book, you will learn about

- **why we measure**

- **what we can measure**

- **units of measure**

- **different measuring tools**

and much more!

We measure things to find out how big they are.

We can measure almost everything.

How much does your dog weigh?

How tall are you?

How much milk do you want?

You can measure all these things!

We can use simple things to measure.

We can use our hands. We can use a cup. We can even use a paperclip! Each of these things can be a unit of measure.

You always need to say which unit of measure you are using.

Let's measure a carrot. This carrot is seven long. Seven what long? This carrot is about seven paperclips long.

Let's measure some water. This bucket holds ten. Ten what? Ten cups of water!

Now measure a desk with your hands.

Did you measure about six or seven hands wide? Did you measure about ten hands long?

Find a grown-up to measure the desk. A grown-up's hands are bigger than your hands. With their hands, the desk is only four hands wide.

We need units of measure that do not change when different people use them.

We need units of measure that are the same for everyone. We need measuring tools.

How many of the tools on page 11 can you find at home or school?

Everyone can use the tools shown here, and the measurements will stay the same!

Did you find a ruler?

This ruler measures in units called inches. Let's measure the carrot again! The ruler says the carrot is eight inches long.

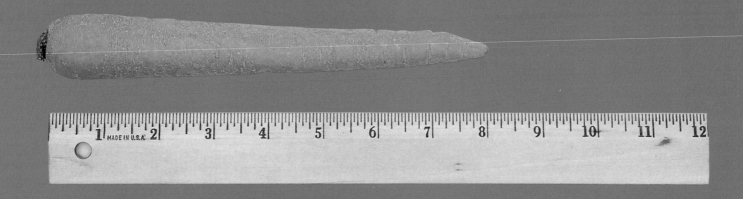

A ruler is twelve inches long. Twelve inches equals one foot. A foot is another unit of measure.

What if you want to measure something bigger than a carrot?

A yardstick is as long as three rulers. You can use a yardstick to measure something bigger.

Now measure the desk with a yardstick.

Ask a grown-up to measure it, too. You agree! The desk is eighteen inches wide.

Choose the best tool to measure things. Use a ruler for small things. Use a yardstick for big things.

Chocolate

Would you use a ruler
or yardstick to measure
a candy bar? A flag?

We can measure this teddy bear in inches.

It is taller than the twelve inch ruler. The bear is about fourteen inches tall.

But how big is the teddy bear's head? You can use a tape measure to find out.

It can go around the teddy bear's head.

A tape measure can measure things that are round.

Do you want to know how heavy something is?

You cannot use a ruler. You cannot use a tape measure.

You can use a scale! You can find a scale at a grocery store. Many foods are measured in ounces or pounds.

You can measure your dog on a scale too. Wow! This dog weighs 20 pounds!

Wet things like milk or water are called liquids.

How do you measure liquids?

Dry things like sugar and cereal are called solids.
How do you measure solids?

Do you want to make some cookies?
Use these tools to measure the foods you will need!

There are other units of measure for food, too.

You can buy a gallon of milk.

You can buy a cup of yogurt.

You can buy a quart of ice cream.

There are so many things to measure!

How tall are you?

How much do you weigh?

How much ice cream can you eat?

Just remember: choose the right tool when you measure something. It makes the job as easy as one, two, three!

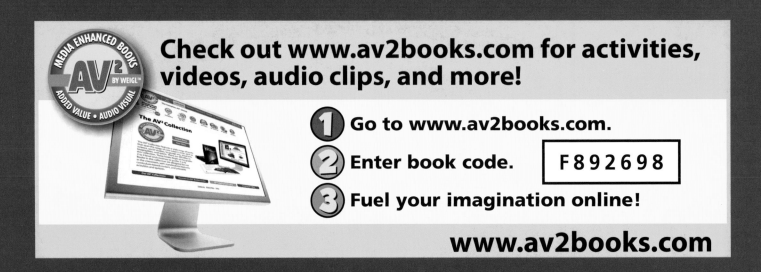